*Coming Close to*

—————————————————————————————————

*the earth*

# BOOKS BY ROD McKUEN

POETRY
*And Autumn Came
  Stanyan Street & Other Sorrows
  Listen To the Warm
*In Someone's Shadow
  Caught In The Quiet
  Fields of Wonder
*And To Each Season
  Come To Me In Silence
  Moment To Moment
*Celebrations Of The Heart
*Beyond the Boardwalk
  The Sea Around Me . . . The Hills Above
  Coming Close To The Earth

COLLECTED POEMS
  Twelve Years Of Christmas
*A Man Alone
  With Love . . .
*The Carols of Christmas
  Seasons In The Sun
  Alone
  The Rod McKuen Omnibus
  Hand In Hand

PROSE
  Finding My Father

COLLECTED LYRICS
*New Ballads
*Pastorale
*The Songs of Rod McKuen
  Grand Tour

*Not published in the United Kingdom

# ROD McKUEN

## *Coming Close to*

---

### *the Earth*

ELM TREE BOOKS
HAMISH HAMILTON · LONDON

'So soon      it passes
our earthly renown'

Thomas À Kempis
*The Imitation of Christ*

This is a book for
BRIAN STONE,
but not about him.

It is his because
he taught me
fences can be
broken. Even mended.

# Contents

## Author's Note

History, biography, science, words strung together as poetry are each in their own way self-indulgent. The writer ought to have an ego large enough so that when he feels it's time to mail, hand over, push forward or let go of his words he can do so, never looking back. Writers for the most part don't have folks to talk to. Probably the knowing or unknowing autobiographer has the easiest and best form of catharsis. In committing something of his life to the empty page he faces every day, he finds an out and in-put, becoming the psychiatrist and patient too.

With few exceptions the words within these pages happened in the year just past. What life I talk about is as real and true to me as I can set it down without injury or hurt to anyone I care about.

*Rod McKuen*
*Long Island, N.Y.*
*July, 1977*

9

# Early in the
Earth

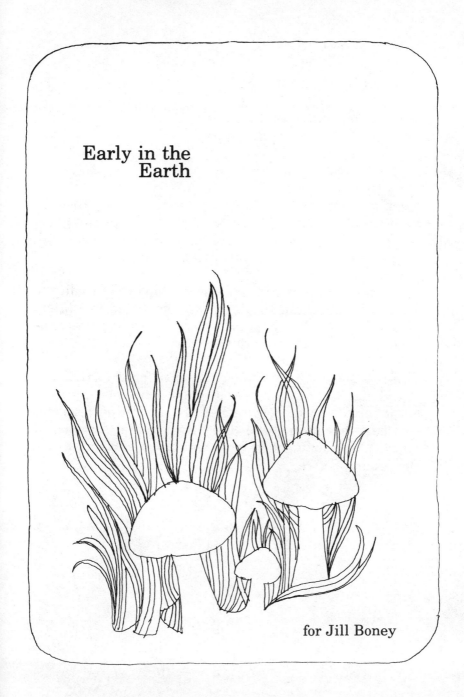

for Jill Boney

## CONTINUATION

*My head is turning slowly*
*now unhurried like this April day.*
*I expect that in the year*
                    *yet upcoming*
*I will somewhere, if not here,*
                    *once again sleep warm.*

Sleeping's everything. It keeps the voluntary thought from forcing out the fantasy so that each of us can go on caring in safety. Yet our hopes and our illusions, though they be disguised as dreams, are real all the same.

As I fall into slumber I'll use the passage from reality to sleep as a means of thinking out the times I've lately passed through. Making ready for what I now perceive as something coming through the mists to me.

This new sleep will be of short duration, for when the roots of hollyhocks and this year's bulbs penetrate my new-found care I'll awaken, refreshed, if not renewed, ready for the next beginning, the rehearsal coming up or yet another re-enactment of whatever came or didn't above the ground before.

## REACH DOWN

Reach down
and grasp a handful
of good earth
you will have touched
the toe of God,
the arteries of angels.

Best of all
by coming closer
to the earth
you'll see yourself
or how you will be.

## COMING CLOSE

I wanted so
to bend the bough
but never once
to break the branch.

I hoped
that I might see
the blossoms
     fall intact
without the petals
          coming loose
or even once detached.

What I wanted most
     was love
in a straight
straightforward way.

I wanted you
not as you could be
had I made you up
but the way I found you
no different from
the way you really are.

I thought by now
we might have earned
a chance to come down close
and lie against the earth.

But I'm convinced
the earth will not allow
even its truest lover
to belong to it
now or straight away.

I cannot care
a little for you.
I love you only just enough
to love you all the way.

## HE

I've memorized my face so well
I need no mirror when I shave.
And so I know that I could not
            cannot compete
with what your ever watchful eye
has told me that you need.

I only hope that when *he* walks
down from whatever place
he's just now hiding
your true love stays
          not only true
but the image of what you
          will go on needing.

If I am not
to be the one
I'll settle for no less
than some assurance
that the ploughboy, cowboy
          or the soldier
the helper or the helping hand
          the final man,
is the one that you deserve
to serve you and for you to serve
throughout the days remaining
          in your life.

## DINOSAURS

A string untied
needs tying up.
As every empty space,
to merely prove
its own existence,
needs walking through.

While mystery is a mainstay
the lack of knowledge
on a chosen subject
needs the miner's pick,
the mason's trowel
and the astronomer's
strict surveyor's gaze.

Dinosaurs
once walked the earth
          but where?
I haven't been there.

How many comets
      have I charted
as they arched across
the winter sky, then fell?
None has fallen
near enough for me to see
the well it dug on impact.

If I travelled
every hour of every day
through the second half
of my own lifetime
there would still be spaces
I'd have liked to fill
if only for an hour.

Some things demand
a finding out
as some loose strings
            need tying
and so a map is brought out
x'ed and circled and gone over.

# EARTH

Alive, awake
we anguish for the dead
we wail and weep.
But it is for ourselves
                    that tears
and tearing at the heart
                        is done.

We do not grieve
because the earth
reclaims its own.
We weep because
we're suddenly deprived
of good companions
        sound judgment
and familiar counsel.

## MORE WINE

Drunk I love you
sane or sober
until the wine of wanting
passes from the vintage
            to the dregs.

And as the carpenters
and the village vintner's son
make up the casks again
aiming for some year ahead,
we fill ourselves
with one another,
vintage wine enough.

How can the wine
of my ambition for you
            be enough?
I wish you heady harvests
not once but four times
            every year
and earth enough
when you're in cities
to make the valleys
            of New England
and all the greenest hills
            in France
stay forever green
inside your heart.

I think
the vessel's changing course.
Where it's bound for
                  I'm not sure
but it will go on
plowing through the sea
till every sea's been sailed.

Call me. Write me.
Send a message in a bottle.
I'll be within the next port
                        waiting
always in the harbour.

*Prowling*

for Doris Worth

HEADLIGHTS

I believe that every time we love or try to love, unconsciously we seek out duplicates, probably with help from someone else because the cloning is not always obvious. Then again there are those rare times when opposites like magnets pull us forward. This was such a time.

## NOON AGAIN

Your thighs
are like a hidden
          honeycomb
as we move
closer now.

How is it that the bee
has left your legs
          untouched
surely he can smell
the sweetness
          waiting there.

I open them
          with pride
before the sun.
Spread them wider still
so that every ray
of sunlight catches them
drinks them in
as I will soon.

You rub your belly
like Italian women
kneading bread
as I move down
between your legs
          closer still
but not as close
as I will finally be
before the noon
            takes over.

God, has clover
ever smelled as sweet
as your warm body
growing warmer still.

Slowly now
I'll be easy
but I want to fill you up
fuller than I've filled myself
with drink or eating.

Breast to breast
        then down
between your thighs
                once more
a sweet triangle
bringing certainty
into my life.

Don't move.
I'll make the motions
            wide enough
to take us both
beyond the sun
and back again
to focus on your eyes.

## SAFEKEEPING

I'm 'Puss 'n' Boots',
or battered tom
    in every alley
till you look at me.
Then I curl up
becoming some grand
    Persian prince
or Eliot's menagerie.
Or every animal
    out in the cold
who happened on
an open doorway shouting
                *sanctuary*.

## NINE LIVES

Welcome home.
The cat remembers.
What kept you?
Never mind,
you're here.

## ATLANTIC AND PACIFIC

Two cats adopted us
one black and white
the other white and black.

You never cared for cats,
                  not really,
but I am ever grateful
that you indulged
my need for pastoral
that kitchen cats provide.

You silently forgave
their traipsing
          and trespassing
in and out of windows,
playing on the stairs
and drinking all the cream
                    you'd hidden
for your morning coffee.

By that toleration
and your tales of Saki's Tobermory
you spoke great volumes
of your love for me.

By your willingness
to learn about
and then be captured
          by a cat
you proved that even
after half a lifetime
of finding your own way
you still could help invent
a brand new common ground.

Two cats
one black and white,
another white and black.
No matter what
another book or bible says,
you have mastered shadings.
You know that greys exist.

Two cats.
The black and white one's
          called Atlantic
the white and black, Pacific.
Since both oceans
separate us far too often
I fantasize that when I'm gone
one the other trods through
          Little Venice
and comes home to you
to lie contented through the night
          at our bed's end.

Two lives.
And whatever comes and goes
through the garden
              or the window
they could not be closer
even at a distance.

Still for those minutes
once or twice a week
when doubt brought on by need
                comes by,
leave the window open
so Atlantic and Pacific
can ebb and flow
in their natural course.

## FORTY/FORTY

Your dress is riding now
up above your knees.
Your thighs
are round and growing
as we settle on the common
my eyes go on avoiding yours,
they move down past
                your body
settling now upon the top part
                of your legs
            the covered
or even the uncovered part.

They move
and keep on moving
trying to find a butterfly
a fly ball or an ocean.

Anything
to keep my mind
away from what I need
                what I want to do.

It doesn't work
we're in the bedroom, still.
My head is haunted,
            turned around.
Can I go on waiting
            and how long.

The park is sunny,
            pigeon territory
can't we move
back up the stairs
where comfort is the main
                  concern?
You know the sun
hangs lower by the minute
its only thought in mind
to give you one more
                  headache.
I'll run
and get an aspirin
the tallest glass
      of water.

Come with me
both of us have had
            the sun,
our share of stale air
            awaits within.

*Hotel
Ansonia
Poems*

for H. F.

## FROM A NOTEBOOK

I've started keeping notes so that I'll remember how it's happening and happened. Not everything is sad, there are the high times too. But usually I get so high on you that I forget while good things happen, to put them down.

## MARCH, FRIDAY

I lugged a brand new phonograph – purchased just that day – some records bought at every port of entry we stopped at as we travelled down the bright Dalmatian Coast. There were even new tapes I was proud of, unheard by anyone but me, made up especially for the guest of honour at your party. The taxi driver wouldn't even help unload the boxes from the cab. The desk clerk didn't seem to know if you lived there as I came into the lobby, and the boxes were cumbersome and heavy. A kind man stopped asking, no insisting, he could help. He did. Up the elevator we came, loaded with the boxes even to your door.

It was then that I felt foolish trying to ensure your party, quiet music. I had erred. No matter what you asked or said. I might have been a hawker selling Tupperware or taking orders for the latest Avon goods. Your friends, I knew but one or two, before that night, were careful with me or at least were kind.

Mostly they ignored me – in self-defence, I think.

Tired, I was, and sleepy. You said 'We'll just stay here.'

Later, could half an hour have passed? I watched you looking, then disappearing in the kitchen with a man I hadn't seen before. A boy, really. He was new to both of us but I could clearly see your eyes were settled on *that* target, that night.

42

Magnanimously, though I will always wonder why, I asked if things might not be better, if instead of staying I journeyed back to my hotel alone. The *yes* came out of you so fast it might have been cathedral bells all set to ring.

I didn't cry or yell or pretend that I was anything but company. How boring that would be for him and those few remaining birthday guests. Instead, I sat down for a time, not missed, but wondering how to make a decent exit dragging all those boxes out the door again.

While I was waiting, thinking, I was really hoping you might pass by once again and in your quiet voice say, *Stay*. It didn't happen and the loading up began. Before I left I wrote some words in a book I'd sent you months ago – one that hadn't even been cracked open. It sat there virgin with a dozen others, all made with special dedications.

*How can there be an ending when nothing of importance has begun?*
I wrote that in the book, went out the door, down the hall into the elevator through the lobby to a corner taxi and disappeared past Lincoln Center. Too numb to even think that I was going home. Alone yet one more time and it would be the last time I would see you, or so I thought, and in that time I wanted to believe that it was over finally. Done.

## WINDOW BLIND

To write about you
        isn't easy.
Compare it to a blind
that on its spring
flaps up to smash
the window casing.

To praise or talk about you
would do more injury
        than compliment.

I try hard now
to remember
all the good times.
There were some.
Sun in California,
mid-Manhattan corridors
and hotel beds,
a Sunday walk
within Miami's mall.
Island nights
of fireflies and lightning.
But everything that happened
glorious or good
must have slipped away
and gone.

The diary is more
a stack of blotted paper
than an abject portrait
painted out of love,
still in a year together
you never once
left my thoughts
nor have I considered
lifetimes to be anything
but synonymous with you.

# CHANGES

Even if I could conquer
muzzle or throw off
    jealousy and pride
I doubt that we could maybe
even find a meeting place.
How can something
come from nothing?

There is the envy,
        to be like you.
To take a soper
       or a half
and just hang easy
while you compound lies
and know I know it.
That would be the optimum,
the top and bottom
the in most in between.

Caught in my love for you
          I dangle there
not so much in space
as the lack of it.
Once caught, I should have said,
for no love lives now
not even pity
or a hurt.
Only the numbness
afterward and after
          any kind of love.

I run home to sleep
while you seek out
your Biblical David.
Your staff and crutch,
inexpensive for you,
because I doubt
that pain has ever
cost you anything.
At least not very much.

## BADLANDS

What you're buying,
                    trolling for,
in The Badlands
every summer Sunday
I could give you
if you'd let me try.
Even mystery, I swear.
You've but to learn
that mystery and magic
are only sleight of hand.

Stand still long enough
to let me prove to you
an update on your life's
                    in order.
There ought to be
            a plan.

Nole accuses me of worry.
Now I understand his reasoning.
It's hard for him to see his friends
worry over nothing.
I should leave you to yourself, he says
but how can I look on
as you allow your life
to flow along the gutter
and disappear towards the nearest drain.

How can I have loved
                    or love you
and not care
that what I loved
not only slipped from me
but daily slides from its own self.

I've seen your room one week only
yet if you were not sleeping
you'd know all the rooms
within my house
your *new* house
            by heart
and maybe each compartment
                in my head.

My friends have started
calling it *the bull pen*
because it has an open door
to Tauruses
        of a kind persuasion.

You'd better go
                and soon.
I can't live sanely
on so many lies,
not even on the truth
of words not promised
let alone not said.

Go.
The one
who looks back first
is not the weaker one
                the fool only.

## MOVIES

You look out at me
from screens now wider
than the widest discard bed,
folding over and over
into strange men's arms
bounding down,
             then up again.
Is there no part of them
that you're afraid to touch?

Your outside climaxes
resemble nothing
more or less
than the drippings
of a drizzling fountain.

I know that strangers
sitting solitary
in shade-pulled rooms,
pants unzipped
or standing, lying
rolling in a ball
            of darkness
feel for those
twelve odd minutes
that you're their private
pleasure, treasure chest.

I am able now
to watch detached
outside myself
not wishing it were me
being taken up into
the warm insides of you
where I've lived
so many times before.

I admit
the first time wasn't easy
seeing you in living colour
whether you were living through
imagination or reality.

But finally
your body reaching out to me
from that so silent screen
became not real
but more a flower
narcissus-like,
some kind of curiosity.

Once I wanted
          to walk with you
down every well-lit street
                    in every city
so that rumours start to sound
                          resound
around the two of us
ensuring no mistake
on the part of those
who live on fantasies
            their own
or those that you
provide for them:
that you belong to me
and we belong, are strong,
                    together.
But are we?

Now you show me
magazines and literature
from here and France
saying you're worth
one hundred dollars
each time out.
I do not find the price offensive,
only that I once committed
the offence.

## TARGET PRACTICE – REVISITED

I'm not sure
if I hit the target
or the target turned,
aimed itself and fired at me.

We connected
in the New York winter,
over again and over again
proving that the aim
was sure and true
or that adversaries
can be controlled,
compounded and corralled
at will.

The enemy
can be confused
a smile in his direction
or a well-turned frown
can win not just a battle
                but the war.

Spring began its early reach
              and all of us
went groggy, sleepless
to the docks on Sunday.

Even as we walked
              helloing everybody
the wind of winter
still held on
not fooled by sunshine.

Three days later
we'd be darting
          doorway to doorway
caught by unexpected
                  mid-week rain.
Winter hadn't left
nor had the spring begun
just because of one long
          sunshine Sunday.

Then,
I don't think it was any time
                    before that day,
I realized that I'd been
carried on a cloud
sometimes grey or black
never white like snow.

I was the target
and the aim was true
no one missed me once.

I'm not good at time
            or summing up.
It took so many months
for a single bruise
        to show itself
I might have died
without an outward blemish.
Now the rupture
on the inside
is every bit as true
and tangible
            as spitting blood.

Never step into the ring
when the flag is up,
		the flag is waving,
only when the flag is down.

I wish the rules for everything
were printed in the daily paper,
spelled out on billboards
		ten feet high
or taught to us in school.
Reading, writing, arithmetic
				and *rules*
needed not just to pass
the contest or the course
but to get us through
our time allotted here.

The trouble is
the rules and reasons
keep on changing.

I enjoyed the clouds
but not the wounds
attendant on
		the course.

I thought at times
my enemies were strangers,
caught in a revolving door
of my own making
then not strangers any more,
their aim too good and true.

I suppose they call it
                target practice
because nobody wants
or needs perfection.

I do.
In the small things
the sureness of appointments
                and the promise kept,
the knowledge that
I'm in control
not always of the circumstance
but surely of the stance
so that I can traverse
                clouds again
whatever be the season
unarmed except for one small book
                of rules.

## WHAT IF

Where do we go from here?
*Away* if we had any sense.
Me cut off from all your lies
and you from my pretensions.
That's too easy I suppose.
You demand that we sleep on together
I'm told by you that it would make us closer friends.
I ask that we sleep closely too
you as my love and I as your lover.

Surely there's an in-between.
The sky is not the answer,
the sea has little for us.
The closer we can stay to earth
perhaps the better chance we'd have
of being people.

If we could have gotten
beyond the buildings
and the bullshit
we could have sailed,
faded in and out together.

## DAVID

You were an enigma.
I used to feel sorry
for the trouble
I might have caused you.
Now I know you thrived,
lived, made love on troubles
I was having.

I think you taught each other
how to lie in small ways
how to steal
          the larger things
like feelings, hopes
and love given freely
not solicited or asked for.

I see you both
throughout eternity
side by side not sighing
or even in the act of love
but telling lies to one another.

I have never been
a bitter man
but now I am
an understanding one.
I even think
you only run
to one another
when no one else
will have you.
That must be
          often now.

I understand that love is not
within your scope
but Christ how you excel
in hate, dishonesty,
thoughtlessness and self-destruction.

You almost qualify
as beautiful people
attractive on the outside
staying pretty to attract new prey
but inside hiding somewhere
is a sketch
if not the detailed portrait
of a masculine/feminine Dorian Gray.

*Windmills . . .*

for Wade Alexander

## MAN

Man was made to try. Afterward he's free to keep or throw away what pleasure or what promise that he's found. What knowledge gained or stumbled on can be discarded or retained. The voyager is always man, his vessel nothing less than all the world.

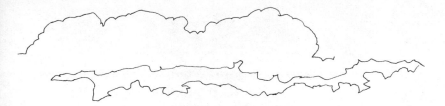

## ON THE WAY TO MANCHESTER

*14 May 1975*

America is tottering
        Great Britain too
I daily read
a dozen headlines,
editorials edged in black.

Countries everywhere
are dropping to the ground
                so fast
there isn't any coming back.

It may be so.
Governments collapsing
only to rise up again
and show another facet
of the same old face.

Vanessa's trekking
to Trafalgar Square
to hoist her arm
and sickle in the air.

Even good John Wayne
              is puzzled
as all the dominoes
                    go down.
It may be so
but the grass
has not been listening.
Apple trees
have gone through April
              into May,
they blossom
pink and crimson still.
And every ewe
on every hill
has one new lamb
              or more.

A bumper crop
        there is
of white clouds
not a single grey
and dandelions
are so plentiful
        they make
each village common
a golden coverlet.

Tomorrow maybe
but I do not think
the world will end today.

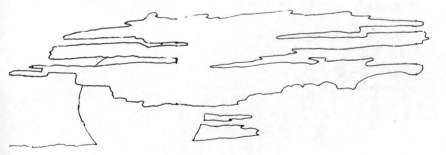

## WINDMILLS ONLY

There are no dragons
    only windmills
    nothing left to slay
    except the clock
that goes on stealing
time from us.

  No one tells
  the would-be Don Quixotes
  how easily a windmill
chomping, churning
cutting through the air
can be stopped
or made to move
more slowly.

Who comes forth to say
the gravelled growl
of these metal
wooden windmills
is only made
by old machines
rusted, needing
oil and care.

The only fire
they ever spew
          or spit
is the glint of sun
on summer Sundays
as steel
slices up
  the sky.

Not here, upstate
or even on the floor
of Scotland's lake
are there dragons
          any more.

Should one pretend
his way into your life
stand back, take aim
              and blow.

Your lungs
are every bit
          as big
as those
of any windmills
on the farm
or in the
barnyard
down the road.

## MY FRIEND AND FIVE STAR FINAL

Frogs croak out
each new edition
as dragonflies supply
the news past noon.

It is left
not only to the morning glory
but field mice in that old
                        fraternity
of sly reporters
filching hill and field alike
to finally flush out
                        all the news.

Better than the radio
                they are
the morning paper
or the grocery handout.

Sometimes I feel
that you invented media
enlisting frogs and dragonflies
as cub reporters
                and as carriers.

The news
comes home to me,
good or bad.
Best of all
from one
who cares enough
to let me know
of tragedies
and triumphs
equal and
with love
so I never
have to fear
the Tribune
or The Times
from someone else.

In the summer months
your well-paid staff
whispers hard
and tells me all.

Look!
Here comes
a dragonfly reporter
                 now.

Too late,
there he goes
on wings of wonder.
Never mind.
You'll see him later
in the re-write room.

# Contrasts

for Maria Lobo Ryan

## TWO PARAGRAPHS

You fill me with anxiety and that is better than not being filled at all. You open up your life to me – could I ask more.

I will but ask that you promise to denounce all those you've known before – even under your breath. I have no quarrel with the men who've loved you, only appreciation for their taste.

## CONTRAST

I know love
by its first name
and living by its last.

I'm not afraid
of what's upcoming
or what has gone before
and if there's nothing
left to know about or learn
I'll review the early lessons
            yet again.

But, please
don't turn the light switch yet
as valuable and friendly
as the darkness is
leave the porch light on
            for contrast.

## PRISONER BEYOND THE TREES

I meant, I mean
to take you to the trees
or the tree country –
as I have planned consistently
to push you beachward.

The trees,
the seashores wait
while I lie next to you
in bed and wonder
will the trees
be tall enough
    to suit you?

The beaches
wide enough and sandy?
The cliffs along the coastline
as beautiful as those
you're used to
on your home-ground
                    outings?

Beyond the obvious
I have no reasons
as to why you've seen
so little of the
            California coast
each time you travel here.
I am not ashamed
to show you off
to anyone and all –
            I glory
seeing your reflection
coming back to me
from other people's eyes.

What then?
Why keep you prisoner?
It could be I indulge myself
by letting only my eyes
                    see you.
It must feel strange
to be a guarded guest.

Give me time
to take your face
                **for granted**.
I'm learning.

# MADRIGAL

Faces there are,
many and few
but none like yours
            or you.

Songs there are,
few and many
but songs are merely
punched out notes
        on paper
without someone
to sing them to.

## SUN SONG

And here's the sun
in case you didn't know
in full flight, but hovering
as if to say, *I guard you,*
*both of you and I approve.*

Why else the warmest
English summer in a hundred years
and California weather
                    you could eat?

I'm grateful
as the year upended
and the English countryside
          grew cold
you came to me
for more sunshine.
I'll give it if I can.
If not I'll make
the snow less painful
the winter rain

just ordinary.

Riding home
from St Giles' Church
I made a new
cantata for you.
All brass and heavy
but gentle with Cuban rhythm.

**THOUGHT**

I love you enough
to let you run

and
far too much
to let you
fly.

## A POEM FOR MY SON

What lessons
did you learn today?
Spelling, sport
          or long division?
Is there homework
I can help with,
problems I can sum
                    and sort.
Anything at all
to make tomorrow's day
in school easy.

With the summer
coming at a runner's run
you should sleep awhile.

There are new games
to prepare for,
some not thought up yet,
some to help replace
          the old ones
too long played.

I like it when
your life is easy
slower than the Paris trains.
Let go some times
if not for you then me.
I'm anxious when I feel anxiety
like clouds or pollen
following through the city
                    after you.

*Dalmatian*

for The Islanders
. . . and then some
and especially
Eddie Rosenberg

STRAIGHT AHEAD

A compass is a small thing, resting on the dashboard or resting in the hand. I'm not sure any compass knows the truth – any more than all or any of us know what's real or facsimile. The needle quivers, points and points in our direction. I'm sure that this coincidence is just that – coincidence.

## VOYAGE

Pleasure is the best
of all things possible,
but for those few moments
              stolen or a gift
the payback is so difficult
that I doubt any of us
would go forward into joy
if we knew the price.

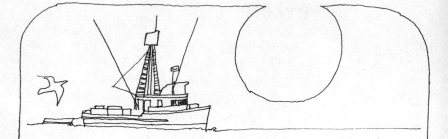

Nole sails down
the Dalmatian coast
and we trip on behind him.
No nightmares on this
            ten-day dream,
where everything is nothing
and nothing might be everything
if we knew how to chase it
to its final hiding place
and bring it back again.

## COMPASS
for M. R.

Though I've been
      an islander
most all my life,
I could sail
around the world on *yes*,
if you'd once use it.

How long should I wait?
How long can I wait?
As long as it takes
for you to master
north and south
and all the other
mathematical gadgetry
contained within a compass.

## FOR TWO FRIENDS

Norman will take care of you
I've no fear of that.
But will you do your share,
make his breakfast
sometimes in the morning
buy his ties and underwear.

I used to wonder if I'd like
the other bookend,
when I discovered
you were only half.

Now that I have met
        the second part
my allegiance is undivided
I could not separate you
            in the dark
nor would I.

And I'd fight off
the unexpected thief
or mere intruder
who carried either of you
down the elevator and away.

You are my friend
          not friends,
the sum of equal parts.
Now that I've met you both
                    I know
your chemistry, inhaled
or made by the master maker
would not work
one without the other.

## MONDAY LETTER: Marine Log

Your letter read
two times, no three
surprised me only
that you took the time
        to write it.

Perhaps it was a form
that you'd composed before,
something to be set down quickly
as you raced toward
tomorrow and the landing.
A marine log maybe.

I found it
half past noon
not soon enough
to question you
but late enough
to keep from calling
down the boardwalk
*hello out there*
*I'm pitiful and sorry.*

*Pitiful* that I need
friendship bad enough
to look for it
from those who live their lives
at such a speed
they seldom make
an understanding pause.

*Sorry*
because my mistakes
are many and uneven.
Even so, *hello out there*
               I wish
you knew me better
I wish *I* knew me better.

I wish most of all
for both of us
you hadn't stopped
within your flight
to write a one-page
form-like letter.

# THE TRAVELLING MAGIC SHOW

Thank you
for the magic show
perfect to the last detail.
Flowers, fish and tambourines
side-show scenes
I might have missed.

Things I would have only guessed at
if you hadn't hit head on
smoking up the subtlety
that most prefer to work out
                    for themselves.

Nothing to chance
now there's a magician
someone who'll jump
in your brother's pants
while teaching him
            long division.

The saddest thing
about a magic show,
            I guess
is that when the final
            trick is done
the gypsy wagon travels
down the road, is gone.

2.
Simple men sometimes have
genius up their sleeves.
A rabbit in the hat,
scarves with dazzling colours
appear and disappear
                    from nowhere
bright balloons from Brigadoon
pigeons, doves and other birds
come from eyes and ears
                    and noses.
In other words, not only birds
but who in life turns out to be
what anyone supposes?

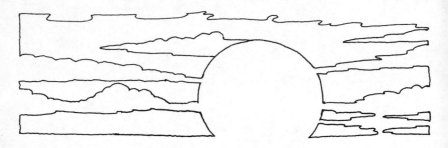

Thank you for the magic show
I laughed and cried a lot
I suppose that's what illusion's for
to store up, file away, then later
remember what it cost
in terms of time and love
                    and learning.
This one wasn't cheap
but I can say that I was there.
Never mind the tricks,
yourself is magic quite enough.

The best magician
I've yet known
is your form striding
down the boardwalk,
turning at the fisherman
then bounding through
        the bullpen gate –
on your normark
corralled for yet
            another weekend.

Hurry, hurry
it's not just
the weekend
     magic dust
you roll and sprinkle.
I need your head
to help in cleaning out
the cobwebs filling up
          my own.

# *Concrete*

for Patrick Devosjoli

## EARTHBOUND

Each of us is earthbound, coming from the stars or wading to the shore. Sailing out, we must sail back – even if the voyage stops upon the ocean's bottom or beyond the universe.

If there is rest at all, we take our ease not on some distant star or in the middle ocean. The notion that the earth is merely a departing place is hardly worth the time it takes to say so. Heaven, even hell, may fire our imagination, but surely ground and ground alone is home.

If we make space within our heads and hearts, then we should take care to arrive at each and every space we seek, together. Dialogue cannot be broken. Communication lines must not be upended or pulled down.

## SEVENTY-SEVENTH STREET, 1977

Women in doorways
breasts heaving heavy
slow – sometimes not at all.
The first long day of spring
has beat, confused them all.

Newspaper fans
spread out and twittering
say whatever must be said,
the women make no words.

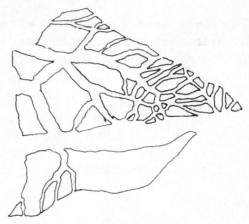

Bare-bellied men
staring out,
hanging out,
of second-storey windows
scratch themselves,
pat their stomachs.

Will the weather break?
Everyone says *no*,
even subway trains
coming from the ground,
      now overhead,
         agree.

Babies go on
crying in their cradles,
kids on play streets
open fire hydrants
and soak themselves.
Adults look on in envy.

*Ready or not*
*here I come.*

A hundred thousand
grandmas rock away
on as many porches.

Now the men
are back again
at window sills
beer cans in each hand.
*When autumn comes*
           *for sure*
*I'll join a gym.*

Today I'd like to know
the face of someone, anyone
I could blame my headache on.

## THE FIRST TIME

Beyond the trees
of what the world
      terms wilderness
there is a first time.
Not to be confused
with anything
that's yet to happen
or what has gone before.

It feels not merely more,
but all there must be
      all there is.

Skating on your smile
                    each night,
I know that I am safe,
privileged beyond
whatever God there is
to watch with you
the man-made stars.
*A Force is with us.*

Away from you
I don't exist,
nothing's true
or even false.
I've no one
to dress up for
no reason
to leave home
or even share what's left to share.
It must be that the learning stops
now that I've learned to learn
                    with you.

## NAMES, 1

Placing my hand upon your shoulder
and slowly with my other hand
taking yours to lead you,
right or wrong or in between,
I care not what the populace
cautions or gives warning –
kindness I'll return in kind, because you care.

Did you know that every hour
each minute given over to me
verifies the feeling
over again and over
songs you make by smiling
jigs you dance by lying still
oceans we cross just by
looking at them from both windows.
Isn't it a miracle?

## NAMES, 2

Right or wrong
only God
dare make a judgment.

Maybe you're unsure
come close then
kill me quietly
unless you feel
enough is nothing or
nothing is enough.

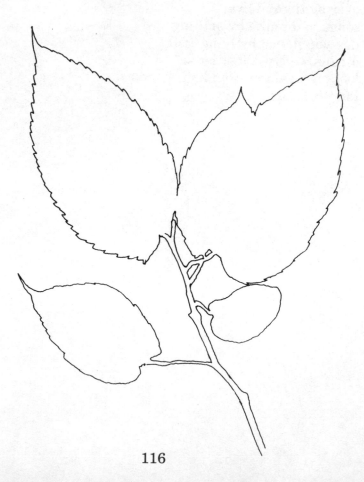

## NAMES, 3

From the top of our high bedroom
I watch both bay and ocean.
Rhymes are absent here
each initial starts a name.

If you read me
       say    so with your arms.
Let loose your limbs
and I will know
needs are not confined
day by day to me.

Promises to keep
islands to be found
nothing can go wrong
everything we need
surrounds us and abounds.

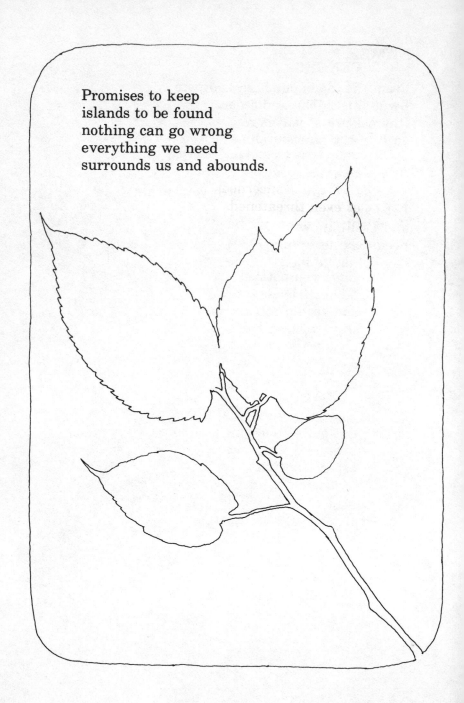

# FENCES

They try
to build high walls,
fences, hedges even
to lock us from each other.
I can't say why
they're so concerned
or even threatened
by the needs we have,
not known to them.

Have you noticed
all our friends
and good companions
seem bent on being masons,
trying hard to make
new foundations –
even other dwelling places
                    for us?
Even though we tell them
our places and our boundaries
are the world,
especially that
new world we've
been building
step by step together.

I am sorry to report
to those who'd lock us up
                or lock us out
that we will not ignore
                each other,
our jailers and our keepers,
                maybe –
but not each other
our own selves.

Let the jailers
and the constables
who abound around us
know for certain
                and for sure
that even if they be
                our brothers
the only true authority,
pistol belt and badge
we acknowledge and approve
is the one or ones
of our design.

Should we be fenced
from one another for a time
we'll live *alone* on short grass
till we're able to deliver
                    bales and bounties
ladles and large boxes
            of replenished love
back to each other.

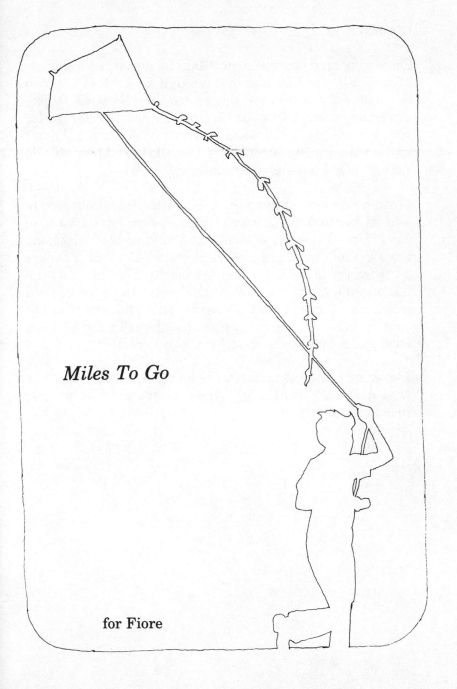

*Miles To Go*

for Fiore

## GOODBYE

Once you said we have nothing to laugh at together. Meanwhile you laugh at me enough for both of us. You clean me out of kindness, slowly, till there's little left. The difference in us, I suppose, is that if I have to change for you, I'm willing. But I want you only as you are. If I don't agree with you, or question you at all, I need help. If I do agree, then I have no opinion of my own.

I said we'd never say *goodbye*. Today the word comes easy and without effort. Maybe that's because I don't have to say it face to face to you. We're at either ends of telephone lines again. Correction. We're there when *I* call. There is no reason to believe you'll ring tonight, after not keeping last night's promises. If you did I don't know what we'd talk about. I only know the conversation, however hard or easy, would end with one final goodbye. The word used with relief by you – regret by me. But final.

I love you still. As much, and as love goes, even more than that first half-drunk night you concentrated so hard on pleasing me and did.

I love you. I am not afraid to say it, even after all the mean and misery that's passed between us.

Apologies are not enough I know. How could they compensate for rides across the ocean and the continent done in tears and not in laughter? How could they make up for Saturday soldiers battling one the other, wounding words spit out machine-gun like. How could they make up for two people desperately in need of one the other not making up? But I apologize for leading you, not letting you love me in your own way – at arm's length. For rushing you, not stopping once to read *your* needs, thinking I'd fulfilled them each time you filled mine. For intimidation – if that's what it was – or being timid and unsure, pretending I was strong when my strength only came from you. For making you think every night in bed was one more potential crisis. It never was. It never was anything but the very best. Even when I knew you forced yourself to bring yourself to me. I never felt anything but happiness and honour, joy and a letting go. No one else has yet come close to giving me that feeling.

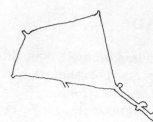

Goodbye. I love you and I'll go on loving. I will change as you will change. I wish you Christmas every time your eyes close. I pray that you will run with deer and soar with eagles, touching on the ground only long enough to find that man who'll love you every bit as much as I do and one you'll feel the same toward.

It is still early in the day for each of us. Despite the darkness up ahead, I know that there will be someone to lead you through the dark and someone you can lead. That it wasn't me is something less important than your finding someone to your liking. I only hope while you were adding to my life, I haven't interrupted anything within yours.

## AHEAD

Who brings home
              the torch
the winner or the loser?
Is the beginning
where the race starts
or is the anticipated ending
just another way of saying
stop the clock
and let's begin again?

Coming out ahead sometimes
I've yet to feel
              I was the winner
unless I raced myself
and passed the mark
I'd set before.
Otherwise I've felt
that competition was just that,
a trophy match
a rally for a ribbon.

I don't compete.
I'm lesser than no man
and I've found no one better.
I know all creatures,
          beings, people
to be unalike.

How can I compete,
win or lose a race
with someone other
          than myself.
Being me is hard enough
but someone other, never.

## LIGHTHOUSE

Because imagination sticks
gets caught
settles in as we grow older
finally there is only
one long, silent hour
even if it lasts a day.

Have we been living
all our years for this?
It may be so.
It well may be
the size of life
is measured by the hours,
years and days it takes
for each of us to turn
within the circle
of the slowest dance.

Where then and why
how does the eagle
or the falcon fly?
And if the rabbit runs
does he run forward
              or run back?

The eagle
and the falcon too
are foragers,
         but self-propelled.

Lucky rabbit
always running to its lair
and always, always
         finding someone there.

I think perhaps
that we are running, yes.
Always away and not toward.

I think that we are looking
not quite for the end
but for a slow dance done
upon the killing ground.

The damage we inflict
in love or hate
or any other name we give it
is usually beyond repair.

What then can we give
or promise one the other?
Ourselves? We try,
but always we hold back.
More promises?
So few are kept
that credibility
must now be stitched
or sewn together.

Finally, the answer
comes up once again,
we can offer one another
nothing but the rattle
of destructive words
a slow death
on the killing ground.
So much for love
        and mornings.

## ASPIRATION

Never satisfied
we turn from earth
            to heaven
knowing we're not
                angels yet
we pray aloud
not proud but sure
that given opportunity
            another try

with one more hour
another day perhaps
a time of concentration
we could rise up
surpass, surprise ourselves
and all of our ambitions

maybe even thrust
an unclenched fist
through an empty cloud
or pass a golden galaxy
and with some patience
and no little practice
even touch the lower sky.

## Notes from the Battlefield

for my sisters and brothers
... those dead and those
still living at great cost
and for Richard and Ruth

Once upon a time there lived a hard-jawed lady, claiming she'd been born again this time in shining armour. For a time she toured and travelled giving other Christians pause, certainly a bad name for their cause.

For a while she received a wide reception, starting wars and funding battles, till the populace began suspecting this immaculate deception.

Unlike the caring Trojan mother something in the lady's eyes betrayed a certain joy, each time she felt a battle won. Sister killed by sister, brother slain by brother, father hacked to death by son.

'Rise up', the wooden lady cried, 'be born again for Christ. Kill another and another' (like I said she wasn't like the Trojan mother, but she was talented and able to sing sharp and flat at once. Making rousing songs of love to God, hymns of hate to man).

Regrouping and reloading, she hid behind her country's flag. Forgetting that this battered banner was woven by each one of us and so belongs to all of us. Just as her inventions from the Bible made up to fill her warped and warrior need have little chance of changing things as long as homes are filled with bookshelves and people who can read.

There was a story once, a fable. It told how people will believe the most outrageous lie when told by someone winsome, able. Until one day a child calls out 'look the Queen', (or Empress if you would have it) 'hasn't any clothes.'

Like every myth, cartoon or fable this story has a moral;
it's up to all of us to save our country's children from the
witch's hand that offers up her poison fruit that turns out
contraband.

To some *The Power and the Glory* is a brittle battle cry, to
me it's just another fairy story. An anthem used from year
to year to kill my family and kin, I cannot help but wonder
why.

As for God, he's my God, my Christ my Buddha too. Who
told him on which side to fight or to fight at all? It makes
one wonder if the Christ she crows about is a God at all.

I pray that she keeps being born again, each morning –
every night, that is until she gets it right.

## BELL RINGERS

Does the bell ring truly
for all and each of us
or does the bell clang only
when the rope is pulled
                    by others?
Swingers of the bell,
            tollers,
bell ringers all
why do you peal the bell?
Nothing changes
by its ringing.

Unless by chance
the bells are truly
rung for God.
Perhaps he hears us then
perhaps he smiles
and finds the clanging
            booming music
to his liking.

I hope that's so
I hope each candle
        lit for him
or our own guilt
helps to light his dinner table.

As for bells
I pray that he hears music
waltzes, tangoes, lilting songs
that make the walks
amid his house
and through his gardens
as beautiful as he
strings out the night for us
and lights up
most our mornings.

## CHAIR

The almost beauty Queen
seems unwilling to be termed
                    chairperson.
A pity that, for runners up
should learn to sit awhile.
A bathing suit
     is sometimes more effective
than a rouged-on smile.

## Manhattan Too Has Stones

for Dan Stone

A SPECIAL STONE

Amid the buildings low and tall that crowd Manhattan, threatening to push it into one river or another, one can find sometimes despite the concrete a special stone.

## DISCOVERY

Hold on to me
as no one has
while we settle
soft and simple
amid the city grass.

I ask that you
stay long enough
to help me prove
that I have worth

worth of some kind.
           You decide.
Am I narrow as the
               noontide,
am I high enough
to touch a single star?
Will I ever reach
the far field?

Do I have worth enough
to occupy an hour
            maybe more
within the frame of reference
            you call time.

Two people living
giving out the best
            to one the other
                a handshake
or a double handstand
taken to its farthest
and most perfect resting place.

None of us
are simple men
though I think
the wise man learns
early on to try
to clean his garage
and his closets out.

I wish that I were
   *plain* enough
to show you I'm but me
or as *fancy* as I feel
your friends all think
   I should be.

Can you carry me
across the water,
turn and run
along the sand
with me
our feet not touching water
   this time.

## PLEA BARGAINING

Help me.

Sort me out
while I divine what's real
   or make believe
     in you.

Better still deliver me
if not to your own self
then to the midnight's
    other side.

I could now be saved
by hearing you say no
as surely as salvation lies
on the velvet forehead
    of a yes.

## STILL RUNNING
(This time into August)

I loom over you
for one long moment,
before I fall
to play
          and plunge
                    and pillage.

I must have been
                    a pirate
in some other life.

If the heart
was truly at its prayer
I think I heard it
          speak a word
make a sign so softly
it might well have been
                    amen,
or was the word again.

You may well be
the one to show me
the survival route
by teaching me the way
          away from you.

151

## WHISTLE STOPS

I know that love
is ladled out,
      unloaded
in the market place
      like bananas
and transistor radios
and those things
made to last
were built pre-1940.

And still I look
not just to find
but to be looking.

A love journeyman,
and traveller after that.
There are cities
            and tough towns
that know my face
and crooked smile
for what it is.

How fortunate for me
the whistle stops
      and factory towns
elect to keep my secrets
as they hold their own.

Increasingly
if it were up to me
        I'd hide nothing
except my face
in private pillows.
For I have almost no one
            to protect.
And yet the cities
work on as my guard
        and guardian.

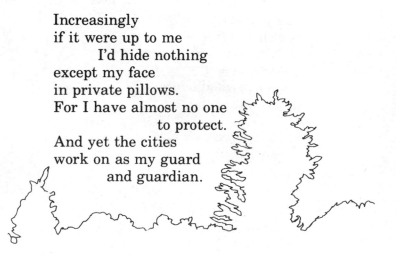

The pop art prize
is still to mingle
         with the crowd
always, ever smiling.
I don't expect
to win the prize
         this year or next
to carry home the trophy
in the year arriving.

I've stayed within
         my rabbit hole
too late, too long.
Perhaps I now enjoy
the solitude
I always fought
so hard against.

What have I learned
as I've gone travelling?
That I'd lie motionless
        forever maybe
or die easily
without some known
        or unknown arms
to wrap me up
and leave me
for the morning's mischief.

I've found out
that I am only
      one more man
trying every way
              he knows
to make it through
yet one more day.

## END POEM

We may not be much
in the grander
      scheme of things
but we're all we've got.

To some it might mean
less than nothing.
But to us I hope it comes to mean
all there is, the lot.

## About the Author

Rod McKuen's books of poetry have sold in excess of 16,000,000 copies in hardcover, making him the bestselling and most widely read poet of our times. In addition he is the bestselling living author writing in any hardcover medium today. His poetry is taught and studied in schools, colleges, universities, and seminaries throughout the world.

Mr McKuen is the composer of nearly 2,000 songs that have been translated into Spanish, French, Dutch, German, Russian, Japanese, Czechoslovakian, Chinese, Norwegian, Afrikaans and Italian, among other languages. They account for the sale of more than 180,000,000 records. His songs include 'Jean', 'Love's Been Good to Me', 'The Importance of the Rose', 'Rock Gently', 'Ally Ally, Oxen Free', and several dozen songs with French composer Jacques Brel, including 'If You Go Away', 'Come Jef', 'Port of Amsterdam', and 'Seasons in the Sun'. Both writers term their writing habits together as three distinct methods: collaboration, adaptation, and translation.

His film music has twice been nominated for Motion Picture Academy Awards (*The Prime of Miss Jean Brodie* and *A Boy Named Charlie Brown*) and his classical work, including symphonies, concertos, piano sonatas, and his very popular Adagio for Harp & Strings, is performed by leading orchestras. In May 1972, the London Royal Philharmonic premiered his Concerto No. 3 for Piano & Orchestra, and a suite, *The Plains of My Country*. In 1973 the Louisville Orchestra commissioned Mr McKuen to compose a suite for orchestra and narrator, entitled *The City*. It was premiered in Louisville and Danville, Kentucky, in October 1973, and was subsequently nominated for a Pulitzer Prize in music. He has been commissioned by the city of Portsmouth, England for a symphonic work to commemorate the sailing of the first ships from that city to Australia. The new work will be jointly premiered in Portsmouth and Australia's Sydney Opera House. (Mr McKuen was the first American artist to perform a series of concerts during the opera house's opening season.)

His Symphony No. 3, commissioned by the Menninger Foundation in honour of their fiftieth anniversary, was premiered in 1975 in Topeka, Kansas, and he has appeared to sell-out houses with more than thirty American symphony orchestras.

Before becoming a bestselling author and composer, Mr McKuen worked as a labourer, radio disc jockey, and newspaper columnist, among a dozen other occupations. He spent two years in the Army, during and after the Korean War. Rod McKuen makes his home in California in a rambling Spanish house, which he shares with a menagerie of Old English sheepdogs and a dozen cats. He likes outdoor sports and driving.

As a balloonist he has flown in the skies above the Western United States and recently South Africa.

The author has completed the libretto and music for a full-length opera, *The Black Eagle*.

In July 1976 two new McKuen works were premiered at St Giles Church, Cripplegate in the City of London. A Concerto for Cello and Orchestra and the first major symphonic composition written for synthesizer and symphony orchestra (Concerto for Balloon & Orchestra).

Much of the author's time is now spent working for and with his nonprofit foundation, Animal Concern, and attempting to change laws in states and countries that allow public and private agencies to collect, but withhold, information from private citizens. He has recently challenged Anita Bryant's stand against the Equal Rights Amendment for women and her crusade against human rights for all Americans, and is a founding member of the First Amendment Society.

*Finding My Father* was Rod McKuen's first book of prose and he is currently at work on the third volume of his 'Sea Trilogy'. He has also returned to writing a twice-weekly newspaper column for North American News Alliance, is a reporter at large for United Features Syndicate, and is finishing a novel that spans three decades.